JAW

Sundress Publications • Knoxville, TN

Copyright © 2020 by Albert Abonado
ISBN: 978-1-939675-98-9
Library of Congress: 2019955487
Published by Sundress Publications
www.sundresspublications.com

Editor: Erin Elizabeth Smith
Editorial Assistant: Anna Black
Editorial Interns: Erica Hoffmeister, Kanika Lawton, Jacquelyn Scott, and Ada Wofford

Colophon: This book is set in Adobe Garamond Pro.

Cover Design: Kristen Ton

Book Design: Erin Elizabeth Smith

JAW
Albert Abonado

Acknowledgements

2 Bridges Review: The 8th Day, Someday I Will Love Albert Abonado
Anti-: The Missing Bridge
Bayou: Bear Suit
Big Lucks: Everyone Just Clap Your Hands and Say Yeah
Boston Review: Flattened Children Are Inevitable
Colorado Review: Luxury
Columbia Poetry Review: Greetings from the Mushroom Aisle
Eleven Eleven: We Are Just Waiting For The Right Kind of Existentialism, Harold
Front Porch: In a Field Called Vietnam
Grist: House of Birds
Guernica: Snake Story
Inertia: On Citizenship
interrupture: An Extraordinary Animal for Extraordinary Times
The Literary Review: Self-Portrait as a Fish Head in a Pot of Hot Water
The Margins: Grandfather as a Kaiju on Fire; The Greeting
Memorious: Grandfather as a Boy Beneath the Floor
Moon City Review: Diagram of a Man with Very Tiny Wings
New Ohio Review: The Morning Table
No Tell Motel: Tito Manuel and a Boy Try To Escape the Invasion; Tito Manuel Meets a Cousin Drinking Water on the Death March; Tito Manuel Is Not Out of the Jungle Yet; Tito Manuel Dreams of the Author in the Jungle; It Took Us So Long to Get Here
Perigee: How to Unbend the Tongue
Phantom Limb: The Future is Now and It is Adorable
Pinwheel: Self-Portrait as a Wisdom Tooth
Public Pool: A Fable that Delivers Spoiled Meat; When One Universe Ends, Another Begins
Redivideer: Postcard from the Valley that I Thought Was Your Face
Salamander: Birdbrain
Tupelo Quarterly: Caesura; The Ghost Root; House of Horses; Frederick Douglass: A Triptych
Washington Square: Brother Octopus
Waxwing: Pancho Villa: Last One Standing is Also the First;
Zone 3: America Tries to Remove a Splinter

Table of Contents

I

America Tries To Remove a Splinter	11
The Missing Bridge	13
Birdbrain	15
Postcard from the Valley I Thought Was Your Face	16
The Morning Table	17
October Poem	19
In a Field Called Vietnam	20
On Citizenship	22
How to Unbend the Tongue	23
House of Birds	24
Snake Story	25
Self-Portrait as a Fish Head in a Pot of Hot Water	26
The Greeting	27
Grandfather as a Boy Beneath the Floor	29
Caesura	31
Frederick Douglass: A Triptych	32
Thumbnail	35
The Ghost Root	37

II

Tito Manuel Builds a Snare for Sparrows	41
Tito Manuel and a Boy Try to Escape the Invasion	42
Tito Manuel Meets a Cousin Drinking Water on the Death March	44
Tito Manuel Dreams of the Author in the Jungle	46
Tito Manuel Escapes the Death March	47
Tito Manuel Is Not Out of the Jungle Yet	49

III

When One Universe Ends, Another Begins	53
The Darkest Sugars Are Always the Sweetest	54
The Future is Now and It is Adorable	55
An Extraordinary Animal for Extraordinary Times	56
We Are Just Waiting For The Right Kind of Existentialism, Harold	57
A Fable That Delivers Spoiled Meat	58
Flattened Children Are Inevitable	59
The Mercy Suit	60
A Head Full of Music, A Sky Full of Smoke	61
Everyone Just Clap Your Hands And Say Yeah	62

IV

The 8th Day	65
Grandfather as a Kaiju on Fire	67
Greetings from the Mushroom Aisle	68
Diagram of a Man with Very Tiny Wings	69
Bear Suit	70
House of Horses	71
Brother Octopus	72
Kiss	74
Someday I Will Love Albert Abonado	76
Pancho Villa: Last One Standing is Also the First	77
Idle	79
Luxury	81
It Took Us So Long to Get Here	83
Self-Portrait as a Wisdom Tooth	86
Notes	89
Thank You	91
About the Author	93

For Catie

I

America Tries to Remove a Splinter

don't worry   this will be quick   my thumb on your palm

your thumb on my neck   my wrist   quick

like your father   like your mother

everything is   a shark is   a wolf is   quick

I have done this once or twice   trust me

If you do not have faith   most ghosts are the color of grease

my hand feels like a flame I put through your hair

I can clip the ends of your toes until they are clouds

thank you for your patience   which is unnecessary   listen

to me when I say you do not need to move

you do not need to breathe   put your hand on my hip

I swear   a quickness   it will be over

and you will thank me   you will not notice how

I have put my hands inside your bones which are hollow

which are your father   your mother   I have your hand

on my palm   how does this feel   the weight of a shark

your patience is rainwater   I have never seen

hands like these   do not move

when I say I am quick I mean look up   the sky is not

quick   but sad and still

The Missing Bridge

I kept looking up into the night
because I felt a bridge
was always approaching

although I wasn't driving through bridge-country
so I don't know what I was expecting to find
except more moon.

Maybe I'm trying to say the night
was a series of stones
or fiddling with the time
I made a habit of mistaking for water
the metal rails passing through my line of sight.

Most things on my periphery are water.

When I say this, I sound
as if I'm rehearsing some stage of depression:
the water stage or the fish stage.

Maybe the night
was a fish I passed under
or the night was metal and the water was me
passing through the guts of a fish.

I could mean the night
was half-rooster
and the water was my brother
and the metal was my father.

I could mean the night
was the sound of me passing through metal
like a trout.

No. No.

Water is when the rooster and man fall
from a bridge and drown
because they stepped into the night
where they expected more bridge
and because no one bothered to tell them
look out for the moon.

Birdbrain

I was just wondering how weird it is to live
in a city full of pigeons and never see
a dead one. I just assumed they must evaporate
somewhere mid-flight above us, probably
into a bluish poof because that is the price
of flying in a city while the rest of us are stuck
inhaling and exhaling all the pigeon smoke left
behind, but then today I'm driving when I pass
five dead pigeons in the road and I think
well what's one more wheel over
their already flattened spines?

I say something to myself about how this
could be the sensitivity of pigeons
or just a day I'm aware of them suddenly expiring.
I ask Catie for her opinion on the matter, but she says
my narcissism is only attractive in small doses
and I say what's that supposed to mean? and she says
maybe the birds are in your head. She likes to say
my head is large enough to contain
multitudes, and I usually don't disagree
so when I kiss her at night she says
she feels a wing thrashing
inside her mouth.

Postcard from the Valley I Thought Was Your Face

I do not kill fleas because I am always a mountain to them. What is the closest you have been to a wilderness? I once pet a sparrow and kissed the top of its head, and I am convinced that has never happened before. If I was small enough, I would visit your body often, I would know things about your body that you are not aware of. You should pay me for this. This will be important information for the future. I would tell you where the clouds affect visibility, or how the moon looks as it passes over your shoulder.

The Morning Table

I'm reading but not reading when I stop reading altogether
because I keep running into lines like *the morning table*.

Not the mourning table, which it is occasionally,
or mooring or moaning table, not mooing, not moon table

but the morning table whose reason in this story
I couldn't figure out. I feel like a failed archeologist

combing through sentences but never coming up
with a coherent history for *the morning table*. Instead, I let

the morning stand for this morning, this house, this plate,
this bread, this economy, this fabric, this egg, this iron,

this bird, this wire, this *this*. At this rate I will
never finish this story, and if I never finish this story,

I won't be able to eat anything. No more milk
or ham or oranges, and without my milk

or ham or oranges, I will wither away to a nub
of a person who eventually collapses

in the bathroom of my apartment. The neighbor
below me will hear the thud of me slumping over

and call the hospital where the EMT will find me
on the floor mouthing *the morning table*, like *Rosebud*

in the opening scene of Citizen Kane, which I heard
may have actually been a euphemism

for the vagina of Hearst's mistress, but I won't have
anything like that to explain my grief,

only that there was a line I once read
that refused to be read.

October Poem

If my fingers had hands, they could play the smallest pianos.

Consider the sound of the tiniest fugue and the size of the ears

that would be able to hear them. Consider the ghost that hears

this and believes the music belongs to the ghost of another ghost.

Consider the room in which all of this occurs, the cat

on the windowsill licking the dust from the wings

of a moth, the colonies of ladybugs crawling through

the walls into the mouth of someone sleeping. A note

to replace the milk with better, more vital milk yellows

in the sunlight, in the damp air. Everything is exactly

where it should be. The teeth are still teeth. The hole

in the floor still goes to a place deep and unforgiveable.

In a Field Called Vietnam

You look like someone I shot once
What bothers me was his specificity:

In a field he called Vietnam where
the one I'm supposed to be is more

of a memory of me who fidgets
with a gun twenty yards away.

He stopped thinking about me until
I was standing among buckets

of produce where he says I shot you
once, and how are you planning

on living with that? In his defense,
I was very tan that summer

so I didn't bother to correct him
with my Filipino-ness. I said

you remind me of my mother
whose green card was stolen

last month. Sometimes, I have
two mothers. I'm not sure which one

was the one I once saw holding
the hole in the neck of a man

dying in a field. I saw the hole
grow teeth and now the man travels

around the country talking
out the back of his head with two

voices: the bored voice
and the surviving voice,

and when he asks for water
his mother tilts his head back

to let the air out of his brain.

On Citizenship

When my mother tells me she refuses
to become a citizen, she means
naturalization sounds too much like a process
that would rearrange her DNA, and she is trying
to avoid the sterile clinic where they would subject
her to electric shocks while an IV pumps
glowing and mysterious liquids
into her forearm. Serious-faced men
in white lab coats would check clipboards
while they observe these procedures
from behind a wall of thick glass. Afterward,
they would lobotomize the part of her brain
that retains the languages she knows
since the group would agree she would have
no need for them. She would no longer dream
in Tagalog or Ilonggo, only English.
If my grandmother appeared in her dream,
my mother would be unable to translate what
would be said, would stand around helpless
until she woke up to consult a dictionary
she would no longer know how to read.

How to Unbend the Tongue

Amazing the tongue that resists dirt
and gravity with prayer. My mother asks

me to teach her how to say *sty*
and *hippopotamus* as if she confronts daily
a glut of filth and dangerous rivers. How

do you unbend the tongue? I tried, once,
to learn Tagalog, reciting a catalog

of phrases into the compressed air
of my car, hold conversation
with a hollow man whose silence provides

its own lessons. What I want is to be
obscene among relatives, to say

blood and dick with sincerity. My mother
told me she could not teach me this:
a brain consumes one

life at a time then bursts. And still,
I hear how she grieves with my aunts, her mouth
full of dust and rice and ditches with wide-

jawed fish that swallow children whole,
that make limbs into shadows of limbs. This

is how you say hippopotamus: a rifle wild
in the mouth, rain against corrugated tin—
weather that ends with hissing.

House of Birds

I swallowed the house with my brother
still in it, so forgive me if I don't answer
your question about the pressure
my tires require just to cross state lines.
I'm listening to my brother go from room
to room as he shuts off the lights, as he stumbles
over his furniture because my body is
an unfamiliar shape. He has a name
for everything I don't know, has given
everything its own cloud.
I worry he will never be satisfied.
I worry he will reach a point where he must open
a window to let the air in, and all the birds
in my throat that have been breaking
their tiny bodies against his glass will pour through
that small gap in the middle of my loneliness.
He will reach up into the air around him and stuff
every bird into his pockets, under his shirt
or down his pants where some birds will poke
a hole into him and try to raise a family.
The other birds will follow suit, pile in
to these convenient new holes just beneath
the pelvic bones. I ask him what he plans to do
with all of these birds, that his body is not designed
to hold so much flight, but there are only more
birds where his voice used to be, birds trying
to replace his eyes with blue eggs, birds unable to find
the exit. They turn on one another, peck out each
other's eyes and replace them with dreams
about eyes. They try to light themselves
on fire, follow the smoke through the nearest hole.

Snake Story

In the front yard, my father split
a garter snake into seven-ish pieces,
left them behind so he could tell
us the story of a snake that swallowed
chickens perched in the low
branches of a tree, the one
the town shot and beat
into the dirt with sticks.
I do not know how one snake relates
to another except for the dying.
My father admits he fears being swallowed
by a large reptile or an earth
that fissures beneath him; even
the doorways that resemble the mouths
of bass is enough to cause cold sweats.
He says his brother once told him
the night was a fish trying to swallow
us, but we were too small to recognize
such truisms. Since then, my father removes
stones from the eyes of fish, divides
the night into smaller, more manageable moons.

Self-Portrait as a Fish Head in a Pot of Hot Water

If you are my father, you will take my eye,
now a thimble of jelly, into your mouth.
You will take my head between thumb
and middle finger, hold me to your lips and suck
what is left, drain into your belly what once
processed light into stories about tax evasion
or the mating rituals of penguins.
You will peel the skin back to reveal
my flaccid interior. You will say
here is the muscle that contained
a dream about his predators.
You will say there isn't much left of the brain,
but what's here is tender. Careful
when you eat around my mouth, how my teeth
can sting the gums. My lips are not intended
to collide with yours. Say this is the source
of our broth, the reason any of us have come
to this small kitchen waiting to become a fire.
Not the beans or the onions. Not the potatoes.
I can tell when someone doesn't wash me
properly, when their stomach fills with my sand,
with the hard calcium of my scales. Listen
to the way the grains grind inside of those mouths,
as if tiny television sets are exploding with news
of another country. Someone is calling out my name.
Perhaps, that is the children who discover me waiting
in the stew and want to know who will do what
they have watched their fathers do for them,
to be the first to smell me in this mixture,
to pinch my dream muscle or tip
my lower jaw to make me speak.

The Greeting

In Walmart or in Macy's, when my father's eyes take
the shape of a moon I have not seen, one covered
in smoke or storm, I know that look, that urge to gauge
a prospective countryman with a phrase I cannot call
my own, that carries the flames of a distant

countryside, whose roads are colors he does not see
anymore, here, amidst all of this abundance. There,
my father and a stranger stand surrounded by the latest
trends in length and texture, talk about mortgages,
about the taste of the air in unbearable humidity.

To the ones who do not recognize my father's call
as their own, forgive him this loneliness, the islands
he thought he heard rattling in your throat, the glaze
on your skin he mistook for salt and ocean,
for volcanos and birds and the bones of giants.

Forgive him the street and all of its fires, the flood
in which his sister is always drowning. Into my hand,
my father shoves a fist full of shirt with "Made
in the Philippines" printed on its tag. Perhaps, we discuss
the murkiness under which such fabrics are produced.

No, the role of the son is not to strip such joy
from his father, who holds in his hand the horizon
as a second skin. Instead, how much pressure
does a needle need to penetrate this cloth,
to break the skin where a splinter rests?

When my father speaks, I dream of the color
of his tongue, how it contracts, isolated,

enters the world already heavy
and blackened. I dream of all
the blood it takes to say hello.

Grandfather as a Boy Beneath the Floor

Their footsteps were an alphabet
I did not understand as I waited

below where my father told me to stay
when the Americans came,

to be quiet or they will find me
and fill my head with voices.

Because I did not want to have
conversations with myself

I waited for them to leave, they
who my mother said have mouths

full of serpents. What did I know about
the language of invertebrates? What words

did they have for witch, orchid, lizard?
I listened to how the mouth can be

its own animal, expected snakes
to fall from them and find me hiding

in the dirt so they could strike
my heel or thigh. I would have taught

these snakes to catch rats instead, how
to retrieve eggs without swallowing.

The only snakes I knew lived in trees
where these men must have fallen from.

They must have been the same tall men with red eyes
I've caught looking into my room at night.

I have heard them swallowing chickens
before I sleep. When they came trying

to convince my father I should follow them,
the heads of roosters were still in their jaws.

What is the sound of a boy
in the dark? *tik-tila-ok*.

Caesura

To learn about negative space in art class, you started
with a surface dark enough to have its own gravity,
an India ink wash, the damp spots imprinted
on your fingers. You scraped away
until the page revealed squares of white
space. In this, one pattern reveals another.
One face could be any other face. The magnolia
could be a skinned goat head, tongued
by smoke. You could feel the coarseness
of the animal's hair when stroked in the wrong
directions, before the men had come
to lead it away. They did not see you follow
them, busy tending their fires, did not see
your face flicker as they scalded the body hung
upside down until you blushed before
the soft thudding heart lost among the roots
of a banana tree. The truth is that the banana
tree is a network of leaves that fold in
on themselves until the plant flowers just
out of reach. You envied those whose
precision with a slingshot could obtain
any fruit, their muscles clearly more taut
then yours, tightened, you suspect,
by evenings that end with fire. The weight
of a banana is one heart and one stone.
When they ask if you know enough
about what you consume, what you offer
to the youngest in your family
say not enough joy, say it emerged out
of the ground one day embracing itself.

Frederick Douglass: A Triptych

Frederick Douglass is on fire. You try to tell him that he is on fire, but he insists this is how he has always been, that he has been building a sun one room at a time. He starts to play a piano just to show you that he does not require any assistance. He is all spark and disco, banging the keys with such intensity the strings snap. Soon, the hammers have nothing to strike but smoke. Soon, sheet music covered in flames fly into your hair, but Frederick Douglass refuses to stop pounding the keys. He does not look at you as he does this. He does not tell you what song he has been trying to play.

Frederick Douglass is a house without windows. Someone has painted windows in places where windows once belonged. You cannot see inside of Frederick Douglass, so you imagine a house full of greasy children knocking over the furniture. A man offers to give you tours of Frederick Douglass where he explains how one Frederick Douglass reveals another Frederick Douglass, the cathedrals are catacombs waiting to be buried. You may think the tour guide is Frederick Douglass, but Frederick Douglass would not guide you through the architecture of his body. Frederick Douglass is an elegy to missing windows. If you peer hard enough, you may find a gap into Frederick Douglass, a way through to the other side.

Frederick Douglass is made of snow. You try to read the palms of Frederick Douglass, but they crumble inside of your grip. When you open your hands, you find your face reflected in water filled with tiny fish swimming in circles. You wonder how long you will have to live like this, careful with your praise, unable to acknowledge success with applause. The fish start to die one by one, until you are alone on a bus with a fist full of dead fish. You want to hide the fish in your coat. You want to know what you did wrong, what you could have done better. That is not the point. The fish are dying. They have been dying the whole time.

Thumbnail

The man in my father's profile picture is empty,
does not show anyone what he has lost, not
the teeth he removes in the evening, not
the proof he dyes his hair, the comb
he drags across his scalp or the litany
of ink around the bathroom sink,
a quiet man with no lips who never rested
his head on my lap, did not dismiss me when
I worried he might unravel when I pluck
his white hair, instead complaining about the roots
that made his head itchy. This is not the father
who did not tell me about the cyst
in his belly until after it was removed or the mold
on his tongue that made his vowels difficult
to swallow, had cast a shadow on the tiles
of his grocery store when seven men pinned
him to the floor at closing time,
before the metal gate could be pulled down,
before the back door could be locked a heel pressed
into his spine while we slept, knife against
the small bones of his neck while men pulled
cash from the drawer, not the father who swept
from the floor the next day everything
his body had shed. My father's head
is not the size of my thumb, arriving
from a country of disappearing faces. Once,
a bird-witch nearly yanked him
from a field of rice and thrust him skyward,
which means everything could have been
different, that my father could have been
a cloud who married my mother and I
would not recognize his face in my own,

no matter how much I thought
I knew about my father.

The Ghost Root

My mother can strip the meat off any chicken bone,
leave nothing but a hinge, no trace of ligament
nor evidence that what she pinches between
her teeth once supported an entire architecture
of feather and seed. She does not stop there,
can split the bone too. Suck the marrow,
the sweetest part. This is how she loves:
offers my father a taste until he too is sharpened
by her appetites. How do they know
when to stop, when the bone has nothing
left to give? My family says I do not know
the proper way to finish a meal, that I leave
too much for others to reclaim, treat them
as if they come laced with a wild poison.
I have seen my mother take from my plate
every discarded knot of muscle and make them
into a rosary. Here is where the ghosts
take root, where the spirit composes itself,
the blood assembling in places light
is the most absent. I watch my mother
work the last scraps, shape her mouth
into something so nimble it can make ribbons
from the smallest nerve before breaking it.

II

Tito Manuel Builds a Snare for Sparrows

A good trap has roots
in the dead.

Find fishing line to bind
a birdleg to its hungers, a loop
small enough for a knuckle.

How many meals have you eaten
that did not contain an omission?

You may want to pull back the wings,
and find the source of lift, to feel
the orchestra of a sparrow's body

in your fist. Sometimes, I forget
that air can be made into a weapon

if it is denied. Consider the garden
as a place to bury your mistakes.
Consider the sound crickets make

when they sleep in your hair. When I die, please
plant vegetables inside my chest.

Use me for soup, feed me to the pigs. Here,
in America, we don't own a field of pigs,
but if we did, they would love me.

Tito Manuel and a Boy Try to Escape the Invasion

Boy, you are fat,
as if I have slung an entire province
of rice fields over my shoulder.
I feel you slouch

into the bullets around us, hear
the air in your chest pass
into mosquitoes. I know then
I could drop you on to

the gravel and you would
understand the necessity
of my decision. I lifted you
because you looked

as if a water buffalo plowed through you
when the men arrived
and you could not find
a single mother among them.

Let me tell you a story about
men made of smoke. Eventually,
the sky takes them and all we
remember is no larger

than the dark smudge
we receive on our foreheads
for Ash Wednesday.
Had you survived, I would

have shown you how to make
our words from smoke.

For now, I carry you a little
further for the quiet

your company suggests,
envious you cannot hear the people
around us snapping their bodies
against the trees.

Tito Manuel Meets a Cousin Drinking Water on the Death March

Since I did not recognize you as my relative
I thought you were made of rivers

because I could taste only metal and dust
and believed you were a body of water consuming

himself for his own pleasure. Forgive me
for not greeting you in the customary way

one does when discovering a distant relative
surrounded by an invading military.

What is the cost of water? Before now,
I had never accused a river of hiding

in the shape of the boy I once watched drain
the blood out of a chicken by hanging it

upside down, but I touched your arm
to investigate your source, to learn

how to conjure an ocean from myself despite
my concern about your ability to dissolve me

since I have become too familiar
with my own salt. Worse yet, you

could be absorbed by the ground
before you could tell me everything

you know about water.
What do I know about shaping

wet soil into your mouth?
Should you be consumed

by the trees, could you pronounce
the names of the fruit to which

you have been dispersed?
Could you tell me then

from which tree
your body would hang?

Tito Manuel Dreams of the Author in the Jungle

On the ground, a man writes with a palm leaf
names I assume belong to the dead. Names
I do not recognize except my own.
I ask him why are you writing
so close to the war?
He says he is building
a house he intends to fill
with rice and lightning.
I want him to be more
specific, but I forget
who is dreaming, if I am
a young man having a dream
about an uncle who has fallen through
the jungle or the trees sharing
a dream about two men whose bones
are eventually polished by a small lizard.
I am often uncertain about
the direction of my dreaming.
He cuts open a fish, draws
my face on its tiny bones, asks
if I would eat my face, says
my mouth is already a house covered
in salt. All I can remember
of my home are the holes. Perhaps,
I was a piece of iron that punctured
a wall, could claim the damage
as mine, or I was the perforation, enough
light passing through me for whomever
woke up and wanted to read
the thumbprints in the dust
someone left behind.

Tito Manuel Escapes the Death March

No offense to the man whose
body I hide beneath, but I am good
at being dead

regardless of what
my urine soaking
in the ground might suggest.

His skin tastes like my skin:
gunshot, bamboo, storm.

As I wait underneath him,
I fold his death into me while I listen
for the Japanese to pass

us. Their cars travel
beside feet who shuffle into
the dirt requests the road does not

absorb them so soon. Such demands
receive no response, only more dirt,
more metal into their soles.

I am listening to
people made of pins.

I have waited here so long
I may have died without
recognizing my own death.

I may have died while walking
and failed to notice the absence
of my legs. This would explain

the ease with which I drifted from
the road and lay among
the other dead.

When you are about to die you are
required to think about the color
of your wife's hair, the mango

you left to ripen on the
dresser, a well from which you
once retrieved water.

The brain blooms
like a full-throated rooster.

But I know I am not
dead when I find myself considering
the condition of life inside

of a coconut, allow myself
the role of a liquid in the white
interior of a fruit.

What is the difference between the last
step to pass and the water stirring
in a ditch?

I will not leave. I will wait
a little longer until everything left is
reduced to a bone.

Tito Manuel Is Not Out of the Jungle Yet

At first, I believe I am witnessing
a small miracle, a monkey
who converted hands into coconuts
so I could drink the liquid.

I do not recognize the animal's
thirst and hunger—I have
my own appetites, the dust
on my lips to consider.

In the markets, vendors sold
monkeys in cages for pets, but
my mother warned me about keeping
such animals around

fire. They eventually learn
the nuances of burning
a home. My father told me
a story about a monkey and turtle

who had an argument over obtaining fruit
from a tree. I forget the exact
details, the origins of the dispute,
only that it ended with a monkey covered

in thorns, a laughing turtle.
I may be at the start of another
story where a witch poses
as a monkey with coconuts

for hands. She once found
a fragment of my nail or hair, kept it

in her teeth until today.
She knows how to wait

for me to approach her,
how close I need to be
for her mouth to snare me.
If this is true, I do not know

how much monkey is actually
before me, but if I wait long
enough there may be
more coconuts.

III

When One Universe Ends, Another Begins

If I had to travel in a Honda Civic with anyone
cruising a dark and uncertain American highway,
I would choose Neil Patrick Harris, Kumar and you,
Harold. Did you hear the news? The other day
the famous movie critic Roger Ebert died.
You made him laugh. When I think about that Ebert,
he is a floating head propelled by his laughter,
an Ebert planet surrounded by silver and neon
while two thumb-shaped moons orbit him,
that always come close to colliding, but never do.
This is the kind of thing that keeps me up at night,
Harold. I keep wondering how two objects can have paths
that intersect, but never meet. How two people can fall
in love in an elevator then separate, and leave behind
a hole the size of Amsterdam. At some point, the objects
must smash into one another. They must start a new universe.
I wouldn't mind living in an Ebert-shaped universe, really.
We would have good food and movies, walking around
with our giant thumb-shaped heads
that do nothing but laugh at the darkness.

The Darkest Sugars Are Always the Sweetest

When you are surrounded by imperialists, Kumar,
sometimes you must settle on the furniture that accepts
you. At least you have a shape for your general gracelessness,
the poppy seeds at the corner of your lip, the wine stains
on your lap, surfaces that will not try to guess
your weight, will not reject your dust. Kumar,
you and I are great Americans. We have great American
hands and great American hair. Great American holes
in the elbows of our button downs and great American
teeth with great American coffee stains. I have tried
everything to whiten my smile. Kumar, I once
had a mouth that was 37% metal, and now I have buried
my teeth where no one can find them.
I did this for good luck. I did this for shame.
Kumar, I love Coca-Cola and its dark sugars,
and I cannot stop singing about its virtues to my wife.

The Future is Now and It is Adorable

One day kittens could become a major currency,
every country trading these adorable balls of fur
for potatoes or Camaros. This is very possible, Harold!
One day we will have to carry large sacks
that are always meowing about the tight
spaces in which we crammed them, the very
hot conditions. I sweat just thinking about
all of these kittens and how they will try to crawl
out of our sacks and we will have to press
their disappointed faces back into these deep
burlap bags where they may tumble around
for hours. That day could be tomorrow. Today,
we fold the faces of dead white men in our pockets,
but who knows what tomorrow will bring?
Fancy aircrafts or a new type of all-purpose vinegar.
I am allergic and will not make it in a world of kittens.
I will not be able to breathe while everyone buries
their faces in the soft bellies of their new
wealth so I wanted to tell you this much, Harold.
I have always admired the size of your head. From one
colossal head to another, it is amazing
that either of us own shirts that fit
the way they do, that accommodate
our ability to be allergic to kittens. Harold,
sometimes I think I am being reborn
when I put my head through another T-shirt.
Sometimes, I look out and can't believe
I am able to see what I see.

An Extraordinary Animal for Extraordinary Times

I cannot stop watching the YouTube video
of the man with a moth buried deep
in his ear, cannot stop thinking
about the wing strokes that filled
his dreams. Kumar, I am anxious
when I see someone pinned to the bed
by friends. How long should it take the head
to realize it is host to an extraordinary
circumstance? How can he bear the knuckles
of the woman trying to extract the thorax
and not ask to be forgiven for his prior
transgressions? Kumar, we grow attached
to the darkness that occupies us, no matter
how loud the song, how deep the well.
When she pinches the abdomen, withdraws
the wings that have lost their soft powder, the ash
they carried into a lit brain, I am still surprised
by the size of what she finds, as if I forgot
the definition of a moth and the shape that implies,
as if, Kumar, the idea of the moth was made
more beautiful, more devastating
when suddenly forced into the light.

We Are Just Waiting For The Right Kind of Existentialism, Harold

Sometimes, Harold, you do things I do not understand,
and that is when I put on my Harold costume,
why I push food through the hole in my Harold mask.
I watch you through the two burning portals
of my Harold eyes and I ask myself why did Harold follow
that man exploding out of himself into a night rain?
Why did he take a stranger's mercy only to abandon
that person in a field of broken engines?
I do not understand so many things, Harold.
I do not understand the shape of the octopus.
I do not understand why asparagus fills me with terror.
I do not understand why my hair was ever cut into the shape
of a bowl. I swear you could stand me on my head,
and serve me at a fancy poetry book release party.
You could pull away at my nose and complain
this is why no one goes to poetry readings anymore.
The food is terrible, and someone always ends
up with their legs kicking in the air.

A Fable That Delivers Spoiled Meat

The field, Kumar, in which you try to find reprieve sits
in the middle of a country manufactured entirely
for you. Kumar, you are not meant to be overwhelmed
by your loneliness but there are limits to the amount
of privacy any of us can demand. If you wanted
to eat a mediocre taco, Kumar, who will love you
in your post-taco life, who will understand how you sacrificed
one kind of loneliness for another? Kumar, we can talk
about an emptiness that spread out before
you or we could talk about the unstoppable force
that is Jamie Kennedy. When he emerges,
his head is ether, his skin the moon. Jamie Kennedy
will not make eye contact, but he will not leave you
isolated. Kumar, you must accept this wilderness
as it arrives, if you want to keep urinating. Kumar
you cannot contain the part of you that makes
the world shimmer. Do not hold back.
That is not a healthy practice. You could get
an infection. You could die.

Flattened Children Are Inevitable

You could walk inside the heart of a whale.
You could have a cocktail party there.
You could carve your name into the heart.
You could pretend to be one half of a couple
that is deeply in love and carve both names
and no one would know about your lie.
Harold, there are children inside the heart
of a whale at a museum, and they leave
mustard everywhere. I am a terrible
person who allows terrible things to happen.
I know about the walls of muscle ready
to collapse in on them and I will not tell them.
In my head, I am yelling at the children, but in my throat,
Harold, nothing followed by whistles of nothing.
Harold, they will sit in the center
of another animal and find it unbearable.
I will not tell them they are the center of attention
and no one will stop any of this from happening.
I will let it happen, Harold. They will make a chandelier
out of their fingerprints and I will let it happen, watch
as the light is compressed into pinholes—
sad, beautiful pinholes.

The Mercy Suit

Kumar, I let the cars pass in front
of me because I am merciful, but I want
my mercy to be acknowledged. I want
people to raise their hands up in affirmation,
to recognize that their passage would not be
possible without me, that they will meet
their deadlines because of me. Do you do
this Kumar, hold on to the names
of those who do not acknowledge
your generosity is a mid-sized city?
Kumar, I used to write names
on my arms and this made my blood
rise. I do not know how many names
my limbs have forgotten, why I can
no longer carry their shapes on my body.
Perhaps all names are mouths in search
of teeth. Kumar, in the spirit of generosity,
I will sell my teeth to those who need it.
I will put my Catholicism where my teeth
once sat. Kumar, I have watched my loved
ones do this, leave behind holes
where their voice should be.

A Head Full of Music, A Sky Full of Smoke

Harold, I am waiting for the sky to break apart,
to finally unlock into more sky.
What is waiting like where you are?
I hope it is not gray and figureless.
I expected the sky to split its pieces into feathers
or hair or hair-like feathers. The hard truth,
Harold, is that I could not look
into whatever substance separates
above us, blue the color of children
who must be taught how to breathe.
What music do children make when they are around you?
Harold, I am told my wife and I will have beautiful
children, and I secretly believe this is true.
I secretly believe we have skies full
of children inside our chests and they swallow
all of my clouds. I am guilty of not releasing them.
Harold, I am not ready. I want to have a star
small enough to fit on the width of my thumb,
but I am not ready. Harold, you understand
when I say this. Your chest expands when you fill it
with smoke, until you are ready to let
the contents of your own head drift
in the air around you.
My children are beautiful, Harold.
So beautiful I will not let them go.

Everyone Just Clap Your Hands And Say Yeah

If I clap my hands together, Kumar, the sound is equal
to all of the songs I have forgotten how to play,
but you, Kumar, when you put your hands
together you can bring a man back from the dead.
Kumar! Your hands are made of miracles.
Do not take that for granted! The stroganoff
you scoop with your hands are now miraculous. Think
of all the people whose fists will never become
miracles while you pull seven bullets from a man
and set each one above you, a constellation you yanked
from a stranger's lungs, snapping that person back
from a cavern full of adjectives for the dead.
Kumar, I placed my hand beneath
a stapler to see if I was born quicker than metal,
if I can stop it with my blood. Kumar, parts of me
cannot do what I want, will not bend
the light in the direction I ask it. I do not call
what I do in the evening prayer but I want
birds to ascend from my palms
each time I open them. Kumar,
I do not ask for much.

IV

The 8th Day

And on the 8th day, God said let there be
Spam and white rice and a fried egg on top

of all that because God knew that shit tastes
holy and the Lord always enters through

the mouth first. And on the 8th day, God said
let there be fish heads too for the neighbors

who do not know how many spines you broke
to get here, who believe you are an ogre

for loving bones as much as you do. And on the 8th day,
God said let there be a house on Long Island

with a basement full of cousins and uncles and aunts
who are your aunts only because they know how

to spell your last name and that is a blood magic too.
And God said a house isn't a house until it is full

of sweat and oil, until someone forgets to pay
the heating bill or the phone bill, and one half

of your phone calls belongs to your ghosts. And on the 8th
day, God said who are you trying to call anyway?

What do you need that you haven't already forgotten?
For God declared the 8th day to be the longest

of all the days, let the sun drag its ass back from church
without tithing, and on this day the mother-god said do not

spit because we had already given up too much
of our water to get here, but you spat anyway

because you are named after the ocean and what you bring
to the earth is a dazzling flood and father-god took

a belt to your thighs after working an overnight and the roar
of the airplanes in your room had grown too loud

while he slept, hovered above you with his god-
breath still dreaming about grease, asked you

what you know about the sky, but you don't ever tell
the gods that feed you how you learned

to let your hands go, how to hold the sun
in its place like any good god would.

Grandfather as a Kaiju on Fire

A year later your body still burns, still sends your skin up
as embers and gives the sky its disposition. When we point

towards the horizon and say this is the color
of our grandfather, we do not know for how long

the night will carry your shade or what winds
brought you here once dormant in a starless

chamber close to our volcanos. The day you fell, dragged
down by the imaginations of engineers, we tasted

your smoke, pocketed hairs that wrapped
our throats, the tooth we ground into fertilizer, jealous

you became a powder that made strangers virile.
Science did not think of you as a body

to bury but a house made of flames. When asked
about the sound of your collapse, how the dust peaked

after your body went slack, we said we knew him mostly
by his fire, by the blood that could not be lit.

Greetings from the Mushroom Aisle

For every vial that contains a saint's bones, there is a corpse that feels less holy. I have lost count of the number of things I buried to get here, what dirt is compressed beneath my fingernails. Did you ever study your hands and wonder how much salt has passed through them? You can wear a suit that turns you into mushrooms. I don't mind the idea of being a colorful fungus, but I would prefer to be stuffed and animated instead. I would still like to complain about television, still touch your leg inappropriately during the commercials.

Diagram of a Man with Very Tiny Wings
after Rachel McKibbens

In the language of children, I don't have the word for tragedy.
I can only insist on the importance of being witness
to terrible, unfortunate events. On a piece of construction
paper, I attempt to explain this idea to my niece
with the following: I draw a man without arms falling
from an invisible building. *This is sadness.*
I intend to explain to her that the man can no longer look
behind him. He has already forgotten the reason for falling.
He can only look towards the ground expanding
as he approaches, except I'm unable to say any of this.
I say, instead, that here, a man mastered the art of flight.
This is a miracle: limbs that move so rapidly they became transparent.
And what about this picture I drew of a building collapsing?
No, someone started to carve a monument of flowers from stone.
Those are not graves on the page, but the names
I gave to my footprints in another country.
Let me start again: This cloud is disaster. You cannot see
all the fish made of lightning that swim inside its belly.
This is where the man falls from, where the buildings hang
upside down, why it rains cinder blocks and furniture
in some parts of the world and every window is a rung
on a ladder that doesn't end but disappears.
This cloud is responsible for every unlit corner
of our home, the figures you don't see that I can't talk about, stalking
our hallways, who don't need eyes or teeth to be weapons.
They are the ones who gathered the dust we left
behind and made it into a calendar. We wake
every morning to shake the days from our spines.

Bear Suit

When I was a giant bear costume, the audience did not know about the three children stacked one on top of the other inside of me. They did not see that one child controlled my feet, another child controlled my hands, and another controlled my head, occasionally grunting at the people climbing up my fur. No one knew about the coordination necessary to operate this costume, the complex signals they made to one another so that the nature of this operation was never revealed to the audience. When children came to sit on my lap, I told them that one day my head would come off, and three sweaty children would crawl out of the deep cavern of my body. This did not happen. This was my regret: I was once a terrible bear, who could not be trusted.

House of Horses

You remember the time you entered a field, having travelled
a long way holding an apple, which you tried
to feed to the horse grazing in the high grass.
The horse insisted, "I am not a horse,
but a house that happens to look like a horse."
You even opened the door on its throat
and thrust your finger into the cavity
where all of its horse-shaped furniture tumbled
out. You left the field and horse-house to gather
its horse-furniture spread among the weeds.
You didn't want to be the one responsible for rearranging
the furniture and appliances in the throat
of a confused stranger. You did not see
the group of children holding balloons
who gathered around the ground as it filled
with dust, blood, and loose teeth.
Children who stepped over everything asking
to be forgiven as they fell.

Brother Octopus

My brother, the beautiful octopus.
My brother, the amoral octopus

who dreams about pornography
but is kind enough to invite me
into his dreams like any good
brother does.

I refuse because I don't want
to be confused for one
of his tentacles.

I want to avoid conversations
that require me to say:

"That's my head
you've been stroking this
whole time"

Our parents didn't know how many
children they wanted
so they had an octopus instead.

"No," my mother says, "You are
un-remembering certain
key events."

Perhaps his body causes me to think
of rooms full of marmalade:

He fell from a balcony once
when his head hatched
into an octopus.

My mother says this is how the octopus is born.

She says this is why the octopus dreams
about its brothers.

Kiss

The grooves of my lips are deep
enough to hide
my parents. I tell

my wife to be careful
when we kiss. Sometimes,
my parents bite

even when they don't
mean to. They leave
when I chew on the collar

of my shirt, return
when I pray, build me
a small altar where the infant

Jesus sits on a bench
and stares at the spicy
food passing through

my mouth. They remind me
I cannot pay
my phone bill with fancy organic

bananas. To everyone
else, I am talking
to myself, complaining

about my brothers
to the clocks, asking
the curtains for reliable

chicken adobo recipes.
More soy sauce.
More forgiveness.

Ask what color tie should I wear
today? I learned how
to shave watching

QVC. I said to the man
in his television suit, he
is also my father.

I wear my fathers
as a necklace: the fathers
I misplaced

in my apartment, the ones
I called for but who disappeared
into those walls full of squirrels,

the ones my vacuum ingested
with my pins, who complained
I let my hair grow too long:

Don't eat with your hands.
Have you gone to church? Remember to change
your oil, to be grateful. Here, take

these onions. I found them
in the road. They are still
good, still good.

Someday I Will Love Albert Abonado
after Frank O'Hara/Roger Reeves/Ocean Vuong

Albert, your name is not your own, but your grandfather's.
I know this does not bring you comfort, but it was not stolen

like so many things we take from our parents. Albert,
it is bad luck to talk about the deaths of our parents without first

forgiving them. We talk so much about what
we have lost: the buttons, for example, that undo

our shirts: the ones we slipped through our ribcage, saved
from the pressure of our bellies, or the cutlery

that cut open our thumbs and revealed another face. Silence
is another name for the love of forgetting. Albert, learn

to love your spine, which is a collection of your mother's
spindles, love the finger bones that break each time you use them

to count. How many horizons have you seen in another
country? How many words do you know for water

and its transformations? You can say mountain and mean
father, if you must. Albert, you want to be forgiven,

but cannot find someone to listen to your admissions, to press
a rosary against your neck. Albert, what happens

to a name when the body is done with it? Carried
into the earth until sweetened, harvested again.

Pancho Villa: Last One Standing is Also the First

If asked, I could not describe the faces
of the ones who danced opposite me,

who tried to make elegies erupt with jabs,
who wished to bust up my face into ghosts.

I listened to what the crowd said, how I needed
to be struck down, taken out,

put in the goddamn ground already.
Said go clean my kitchen.

Said make me rice. No man loses
to a fucking monkey. Tell these men

what I know: before the torque, the snap,
a punch rises from the dirt and I've got bones

made of coal. I'm half earth, half fire.
I'm made of teeth and shine, earned

this space by bringing the night with my hands,
came with the tide slung over my shoulder.

I'm the one who buried Magellan,
who traded missionaries for knives.

I've got each one of Rizal's bullets,
and I've brought them back as fists.

They came for names like Frankie Genaro,
Johnny Buff, and Jimmy Wilde.

These are those half-devil/half-child fists.
These are those 300 years fists.

Maybe I did leave my jaw to rot
for too long, should have taken

the hospital bed when I had the chance.
Didn't they know I already had a mouth

full of poison? Instead, they said
I left too much to grit and alcohol,

and no man can expect to live like that
for long, but it wasn't all about living either.

Idle

A warning to the ones I love: I want to pick

for myself the mucus hanging

from your nose   Call it *Lonely Rosebud*   *Tender Spider*

My mother sits on the edge

of her hospital bed telling me the meaning behind

the tax forms on her lap   telling me how to love

the cousins I have never met   I give the mucus wadded

inside her nose a name   *The Oldest Song*   *Opal In My Heart*

I think it has eyes   sees me watching it laugh

when my mother laughs   I ask it not to retreat

into her throat where it might interrupt her stories   I like

this story   This is the one about an uncle who discovers

another uncle in an unexpected place   I want her

to tell it again and again   dust   wheel   river

What did she call her brothers when she was angry at them?

Would my thumbs fit in her nostrils?   I do not know

what to do with my hands during a story   Sometimes they are

a small herd that climbs my wife's spine when she sleeps

She wants to know where I am going with them   I say

they are lost   They came from a country

full of rivers and no GPS   They wonder what she

will do with all of her bones when she is done

with them   They followed a star here

They came looking for myrrh   This is an old story

Maybe you have heard it before

Luxury

Today, I do not think about death, not
the brittle skulls of children or the metal
in their blood that passes for bullets.
I do not think about the bones
of birds or the blackberry seeds left
in the belly, the time a muscle takes
to go blue from a deflated lung, not the bright
jaws of insects that come for the flesh, the meat.
I do not think of grief as a color
on my aunt's tongue, her face a country
of fires. I do not think about kissing
my grandfather in his coffin, not the temperature
of his lips. Today, I lose count, forget
about sorrow and its teeth, regret
and its prickled skin, how to pray
for the dead I do not have to bury, that hymns
turn my mouth into a sun, that terror
can be the same word for skin or brain, forget
I do not speak Chinese or have to correct
anyone who asks if I speak Chinese,
say no, I am afraid I am Filipino,
say I do not speak Tagalog either.
I do not ask anyone to forgive me
for forgetting and this is the oldest joy.
Let me forget that I cannot hold
the moon to feed it peppers when I want,
that the rain in the trees is not a rapture,
an applause for the rose on my shoes, that I do not
blister and crack from holiness. Today,
I am holy and when I split my lip on the fist
of my brother that was holy too, and when I kneel

in the center of an empty parking lot I do so grateful I can taste my blood.

It Took Us So Long to Get Here

December 13

I said *we walk to my uncle's home
in the Philippines* when I should
have said *to the place my father
was raised* except that wouldn't account
for the fresh concrete in the nearby chapel,
the absence of kerosene batteries,
the plumbing, the number
of water buffalo that have been
lost. I could have said *where
I no longer have to cross ditches,
where I once bathed in the rain,
where I watched a pig slaughtered
for the first time.* They gagged the pig
with a large stick shoved down
its throat before slitting the neck open
and afterwards children bounced
a balloon made from its bladder
against their knees and thighs.

January 3

"Which one is he?" is not a question
I should ask about the groom
when offering a gift at a wedding, but I wanted
to know if he was the one I once met
at a funeral with a voice that reminded me
of my favorite sandwich or if he was the one
with the very egg-like personality.
I hoped he wasn't the one who liked
to speak with a mouth full of meat.
When I dream of that one, all I see are teeth.

November 23

Despite the surprise of finding
my grandfather's coffin in the living room, I thought
the body looked good
if we ignored the heat and the poor
makeup. Granted,
he was kept sealed behind glass so I couldn't
get close enough to really inspect
the body or hold his wrist, and I wanted
to brush from his collar the stray
powder used to color his cheeks, adjust
the hue of his lips, but all things considered,
at least he didn't smell, which makes me
feel optimistic since I'll be sleeping
in the room across from him and the last thing
any of us wants is to sit down
to our meals and be reminded
of a body decomposing in the same room.
I preferred to think of him as someone who got bored
and passed out after watching an episode
of *Survivor*, who prefers taking naps behind
thin glass with a vase full of flowers sitting
on his chest, and because everything
was so good, I didn't think
about the gash in his head. It must
have been like a little moon
escaping his scalp when he slipped
and fell in the bathroom, which according
to one relative, would have never happened
if he had been living in America.

Self-Portrait as a Wisdom Tooth

Should this be proof that I have become
something other than myself, more
than a stone that crowds close
to the throat and its clot
of obscenities, a point furthest
from a kiss, a jaw left afraid
to clamp down on any sweetness,
to bend or grind meat into salt,
then let the head shatter each time
I collide against myself, recoil from
my ghostly hum. I do not own
the blood that passes beneath
me, but I threaten its alignment—
the mouth and its horoscope root
every thread of gossip. Let me carry into
the brain a new wilderness, deer
that shed their antlers in inconvenient
fields. I know the skull
possesses its own starlight.
I know what poisons permit some
to sleep, that rot can be the same
word for sugar, that extraction
means to break without apology,
to say you were never meant
to be in this place.

Notes

Francisco Guilledo a.k.a Pancho Villa was a Filipino boxer who rose to prominence in the 1920's. He became the first Asian world champion boxer, beating Jimmy Wilde in an upset to claim the tile of World Flyweight Champion.

"8th Day" owes a debt to Genesissy by Danez Smith.

"Diagram of a Man with Very Tiny Wings" owes a debt to "After School Special" by Rachel McKibbens.

In the poem "Grandfather as a Boy Beneath the Floor," the phrase *tik-tila-ok* is a Tagalog translation of cock-a-doodle-do.

Harold and Kumar addressed in the poems of section three refer to the characters from the movie *Harold and Kumar Go To White Castle*.

Thank You

This collection owes a tremendous debt to my parents Norma and Carlito Abonado, whose resilience, grit, and enormous hearts remain a guiding force that informs the spirit of so many of these poems. They've taught me that family and community is a practice, that my writing thrives because of the people who sacrificed to pioneer the spaces for my voice and others.

Gratitude to the institutions that supported my writing. Thank you to the Bennington Writing Seminars community that has helped sustain me. Thank you to my instructors for their generosity, incisive critiques, and support: Ed Ochester, Michael Burkard, Major Jackson, Amy Gerstler, and Timothy Liu. Their steady hand as mentors continue to shape and inform me. Thank you to the New York Foundation for the Arts whose support helped me finish this book.

Thank you to all the writers who have been a steady, necessary presence, who have seen and heard many of these poems at various stages and offered their invaluable insight, who provide space for community: Willa Carroll, Jonathan Everitt, Geoff Graser, Charlie Cote, Sarah Freligh, David Forman, Sarah Cedeno, George Guida Robert V Hansman, Noah Falck, Reilly Hirst, John Gallaher, Sejal Shah, Lytton Smith, Tony Leuzzi, Wanda Schubmehl, Ralph Black, Peter Conners, and Sasha Pimentel.

Thank you to John Cho and Kal Penn for Harold & Kumar. I did not know I needed an Asian stoner movie until I saw one.

Grateful, also, for my students, who regularly teach me how to become a better reader, to be accountable to my writing, to listen closer.

Thank you to Spam.

Thank you to Erin and the staff at Sundress for plucking this book out of the pile and believing in it.

Thank you, finally, to Catie for your kindness, endless patience, which is really an understatement, and love.

About the Author

Albert Abonado teaches Creative Writing at SUNY Geneseo. He received a fellowship from the New York Foundation for the Arts. His poems have appeared in *Colorado Review, Pleiades, The Margins, Waxwing, Zone 3*, and others. He hosts the poetry radio show Flour City Yawp on WAYO 104.3FM-LP. He lives in Rochester, NY with his wife.

Other Sundress Titles

Lessons in Breathing Underwater
H.K. Hummel
$16

Bury Me in Thunder
moira j.
$16

Dead Man's Float
Ruth Foley
$16

Gender Flytrap
Zoë Estelle Hitzel
$16

Blood Stripes
Aaron Graham
$16

Boom Box
Amorak Huey
$16

Arabilis
Leah Silvieus
$16

Afakasi | Half-Caste
Hali F. Sofala-Jones
$16

Match Cut
Letitia Trent
$16

Marvels
MR Sheffield
$20

Passing Through Humansville
Karen Craigo
$16

Divining Bones
Charlie Bondus
$16

Phantom Tongue
Steven Sanchez
$15

The Minor Territories
Danielle Sellers
$15

Citizens of the Mausoleum
Rodney Gomez
$15

Actual Miles
Jim Warner
$15

Printed in the USA
CPSIA information can be obtained
at www.ICGtesting.com
LVHW091048291223
767646LV00001B/199